CREATE YOUR OWN
PETER RABBIT™
NURSERY

Based on the original Tales by
BEATRIX POTTER

F. WARNE & CO

CONTENTS

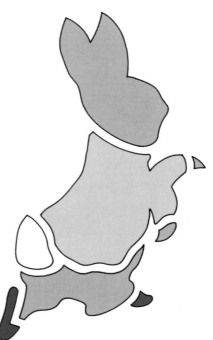
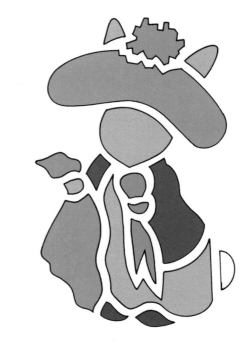
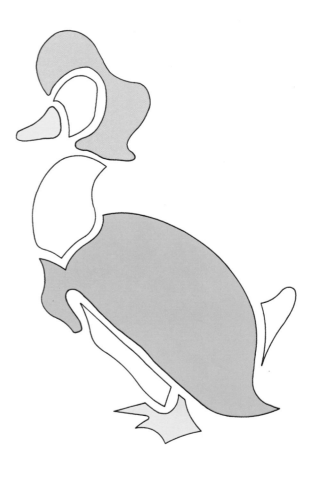

INTRODUCTION

The adventures of Peter Rabbit have been beloved for over a century and continue to enchant children today. What better theme for decorating your child's nursery than the delightful Tales of Beatrix Potter? Peter Rabbit and his friends will help transform your spare room into a magical nursery where your baby can sleep, learn and play comfortably.

Stencil of Mrs. Rabbit putting Peter to bed

Recognising the popularity of her creation, Beatrix Potter made a Peter Rabbit doll with paintbrush bristles for whiskers and feet stuffed with lead bullets to make it stand upright. In 1903, a year after *The Tale of Peter Rabbit* was published, Beatrix patented her toy. The next year, Beatrix designed a wall frieze depicting her characters. She described the wallpapers in a letter, 'We have done them flat, like stencil colours; they are less frightful than might have been expected, and Mr. McGregor is magnificent on the frieze.' Beatrix shrewdly developed many products reproducing her artwork, such as stencils and a board game, but insisted that the designs remain faithful to the original book illustrations.

Create a Peter Rabbit Nursery features a variety of projects inspired by Beatrix Potter's little books. Using motifs based on her characters, warm colours reflecting her palette and traditional craft techniques, this book gives you the tools to create a practical, attractive nursery with a classic style. Written with busy parents-to-be in mind, the decorating ideas suggested do not require crafts expertise or a large budget. Prepare your nursery in advance, however, for you will be far too busy after the baby's arrival!

Peter Rabbit doll patented by Beatrix Potter in 1903

Information on Beatrix Potter nursery products available to purchase can be found on the Peter Rabbit Web Site: **www.peterrabbit.com**

STENCILLING

Proper equipment will help you to achieve the best stencilling results. Round stencil brushes have flat, stiff bristles and should be held straight, rather than at an angle. Choose brushes that suit the size of the stencil you are using.

You will need:
- sandpaper
- primer
- base paint
- paintbrush
- scissors
- paper
- stencils
- pencil
- acrylic paint
- stencil brushes
- masking tape
- paper towels
- cloth
- varnish

Preparing surfaces

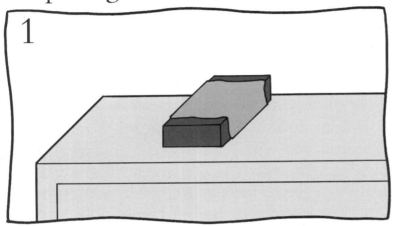

Smooth down new furniture with medium-grade sandpaper. Paint an undercoat of primer, then sand with fine-grade sandpaper when dry. If using old wood, remove any chipped paint before sanding and priming.

For your base colour, use one coat of eggshell paint or a water-based, matt-finish emulsion paint. Do not use gloss paint, as varnish will not adhere to it. Sand down any obvious brush strokes to achieve a smooth finish.

Stencilling

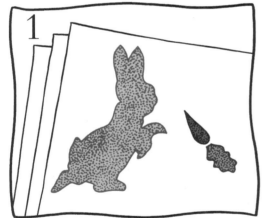

Cut out stencils from the back of the book. Plan out your design and make a few prints on sheets of paper to practise your stencilling technique.

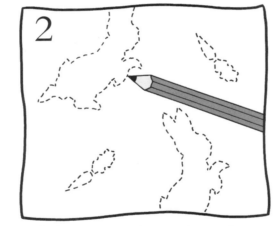

Work out equal intervals on the object where each stencil should fall. Lightly draw around the stencil in pencil to mark the positions.

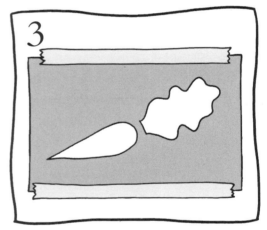

Stick the stencil into place with masking tape. Dip the very end of your brush in acrylic paint, then blot off extra paint on a paper towel.

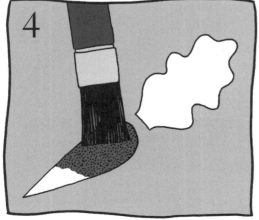

Apply the paint in a circular motion, filling in the outline from the edges to centre. Don't overload the brush, as paint will seep under the stencil.

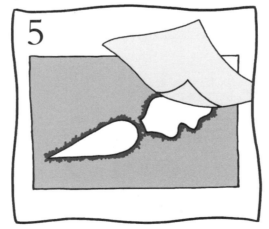

Fill in every section of the stencil, changing brushes for each new colour. Wipe the stencil with a damp cloth occasionally to prevent smudges.

Wait a few seconds for the paint to dry before removing the stencil. When the stencilling is complete and dry, apply varnish if necessary.

WALL BORDERS

Using the stencils provided at the back of the book, you can decorate your nursery walls with any of the borders pictured below. A stencilled border can accentuate unusual features of the room, such as wainscoting or a picture rail. First, remove any dust or cobwebs from the walls. With a ruler and a length of masking tape, mark out a straight guideline for your stencils to follow. Plan around any obstructions along the path, such as windows. Work out equal intervals at which the stencils should fall and lightly draw the route in pencil. Begin stencilling in one corner and work left-to-right (or right-to-left for left-handers) around the room until you reach the start again. There is no need to varnish wall borders.

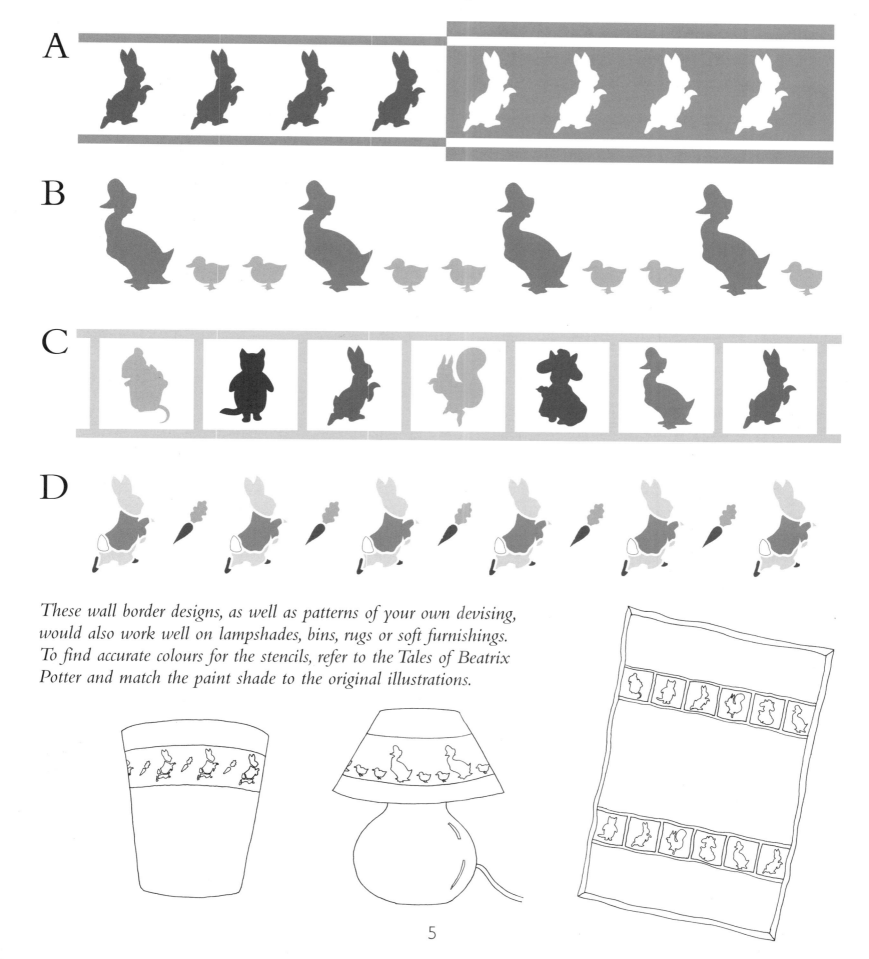

These wall border designs, as well as patterns of your own devising, would also work well on lampshades, bins, rugs or soft furnishings. To find accurate colours for the stencils, refer to the Tales of Beatrix Potter and match the paint shade to the original illustrations.

STENCILLING PROJECTS

Producing quick results with inexpensive materials, stencilling is an ideal craft for anyone with little time or resources to spare. The items shown here, made with the stencils provided, demonstrate the versatility of stencilling. The same simple technique can be used to create beautiful designs on wood, fabric and walls. Turn overleaf for instructions on how to complete each project.

Floor Mat

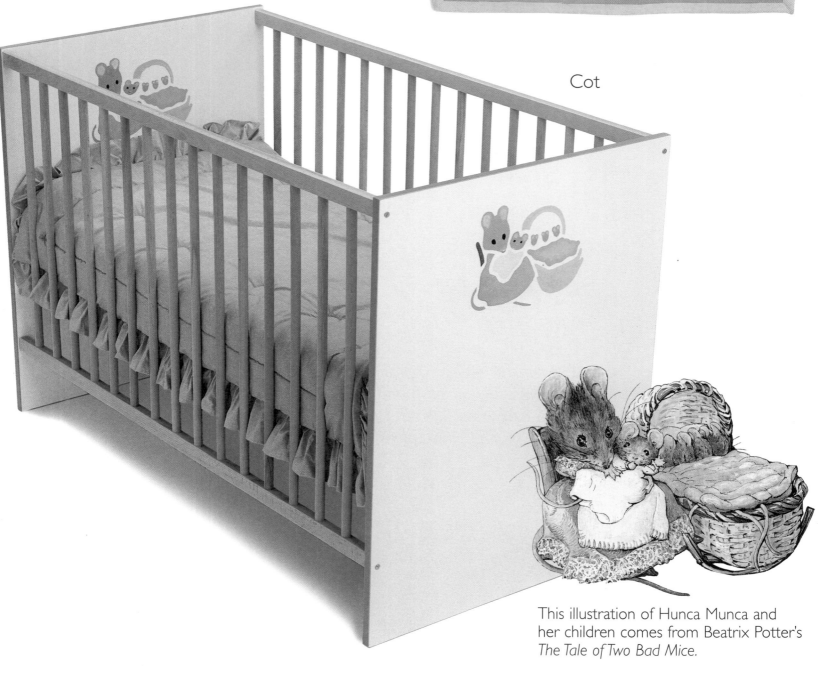

Cot

This illustration of Hunca Munca and her children comes from Beatrix Potter's *The Tale of Two Bad Mice*.

Laundry Bag

Window Blind

Toy Box

Chest of Drawers

Lampshade

WINDOW BLIND

This fabric blind will enliven the nursery window
with bright splashes of primary colours.

1. Unfurl the blind on to a clean, flat surface and lightly
   mark in pencil where you want the rabbits to fall.
2. Position the Peter Rabbit silhouette stencil and fill it
   in with pale blue fabric paint. Alternate the angle of
   the stencil to create a random effect.
3. Using red and green fabric paint, stencil radishes at
   alternating angles in the gaps between the rabbits.

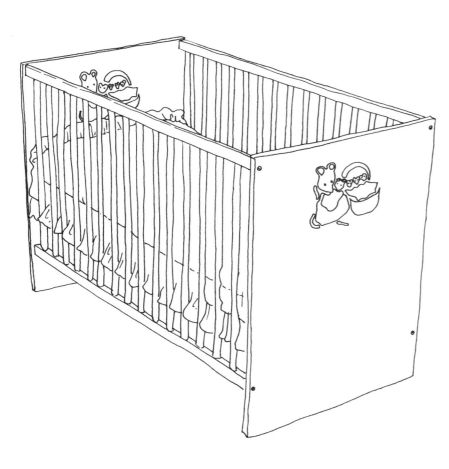

COT

Hunca Munca, rocking her baby mice
to sleep, makes a charming decoration
for a cot's headboard.

1. Begin by painting the boards at each end of the
   cot white on both sides.
2. Tape the Hunca Munca stencil to the middle
   of the headboard and fill in the stencil with
   acrylic paint. Paint Hunca Munca's dress pale
   blue, her body and babies brown, the cradle
   and swathe yellow and the blanket pink.
3. Repeat the stencil on the reverse side and
   at the opposite end of the cot. Varnish the
   stencils when dry.

FLOOR MAT

Transform a neutral, rectangular floor mat with
a delightful Peter Rabbit motif.

1. Using masking tape, mark off a border approximately
   14 cm (5½ inches) thick on the floor mat.
   Paint the border with blue fabric paint.
2. When the paint has dried, stencil the Peter Rabbit
   silhouette at regular intervals along the blue border
   using white fabric paint.
3. Enlarge the Peter Rabbit stencil on a photocopier
   until it nearly fills the blue frame. Stick the copy on to
   stencil card, then cut out around the shape to make a
   new stencil. Tape the stencil to the centre of the mat.
4. Fill in the stencil with fabric paint. Paint Peter's jacket
   blue, his tail white, his fur light brown and his shoes
   and eye dark brown.

LAMPSHADE

Reverse stencilling looks lovely on a fabric lampshade.

1. Position strips of masking tape 2.5 cm (one inch) from the top and bottom of the lampshade.
2. Trace around the Jemima Puddle-duck silhouette stencil on to a piece of paper and cut out the shape. Make as many paper cut-outs as needed to decorate around the lampshade.
3. Stick the cut-outs at regular intervals between the two borders using small rolls of masking tape attached to the back of the cut-outs.
4. Gently sponge pale yellow fabric paint over the lampshade. When the paint has dried, remove the masking tape and paper cut-outs.

CHEST OF DRAWERS

A small, white chest of drawers can be adapted for the nursery by stencilling favourite characters in pretty, pastel colours.

1. Paint the top and sides of the chest of drawers pink.
2. Stencil the Peter Rabbit silhouette in blue across the top drawer and paint the knobs to match.
3. Stencil the Jemima Puddle-duck silhouette in pink along the middle drawer and paint the knobs to match.
4. Finally, stencil a border of Tom Kitten silhouettes in mauve along the bottom drawer and paint the knobs to match.

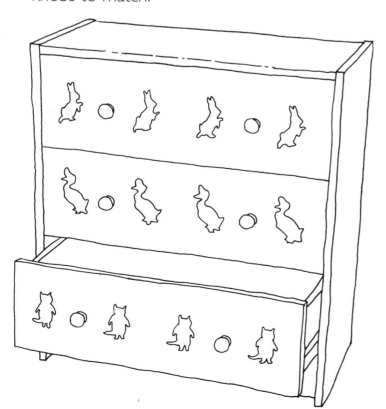

TOY BOX

Decorate a plain wooden chest and turn it into an imaginative toy box, essential for reducing nursery clutter.

1. Paint the toy chest pale blue, with a border of pale yellow around the edges.
2. Stencil bright yellow ducklings around the chest at equal intervals using the large duckling stencil.
3. On the top of the chest, stencil an alternating pattern of ducklings and Jemima Puddle-ducks. Fill in the Jemima Puddle-duck stencil, using white paint for her body, pink for her shawl, bright blue for her bonnet and bright yellow for her feet and beak. Apply a few coats of varnish when dry.

LAUNDRY BAG

Hang this handy laundry bag near the changing table.

1. Cut a piece of blue fabric 50 × 70 cm (20 × 28 inches). Stencil the Peter Rabbit silhouette at regular intervals using white fabric paint.
2. When the paint has dried, fold the fabric in half (stencilled pattern on the inside). Sew in running stitch along the bottom edge and up the side, stopping about 5 cm (2 inches) from the top.
3. Turn down the top 2.5 cm (1 inch) of the bag and sew a running stitch around the bottom of the fold to make a channel.
3. Turn the bag right side out. Thread a length of white cord through the channel and tie the ends in a secure knot.

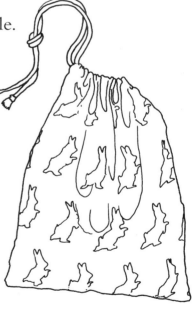

DECOUPAGE

Deriving from the French word 'découpure', meaning to cut out, the craft of decoupage uses paper cut-outs, or scraps, to embellish painted furnishings. In Victorian times, decoupage enthusiasts often used children's book illustrations as scraps. Beatrix Potter's watercolour pictures make ideal decoupage scraps, and there are plenty for you to cut out on pages 14–19. This easy decorating technique can transform plain furniture and accessories into attractive nursery items at a minimal cost. Here are some projects to inspire you, but why not experiment with your own designs?

Mirror

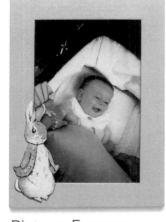

Picture Frames

Kirstie's Room

Name Plates

Andrew's Room

Chair

Coat Pegs

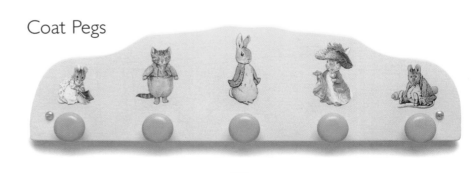

Clothes Hangers

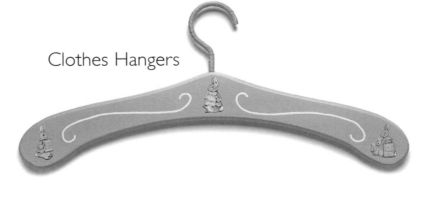

Decoupage Techniques

Once you have mastered these basic decoupage techniques there's no end to the beautiful pieces you can create. Taking time to prepare surfaces and plan the colour scheme will help ensure a professional-looking finished object.

Preparing surfaces

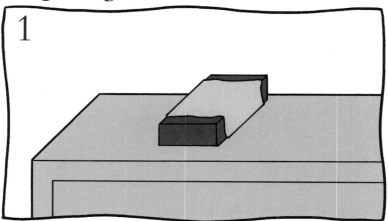

Smooth down new furniture with medium-grade sandpaper. Paint an undercoat of primer, then sand with fine-grade sandpaper when dry. If using old wood, remove any chipped paint before sanding and priming.

For your base colour, use one coat of eggshell paint or a water-based, matt-finish emulsion paint. Do not use gloss paint, as varnish will not adhere to it. Sand down any obvious brush strokes to achieve a smooth finish.

Decorating

After preparing your surface and selecting a pattern, cut out your scraps. A scalpel and cutting mat may be easier than scissors for cutting small scraps.

Arrange your scraps on the surface you wish to decorate. Hold the scraps in place with small blobs of reusable adhesive and reposition if necessary.

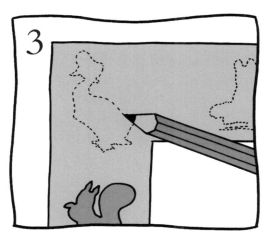

When you are pleased with your design, remove the scraps a few at a time and lightly mark their positions with a pencil. Remove reusable adhesive from scraps.

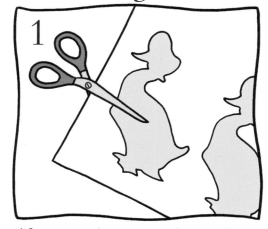

Stick the scraps into place with a thin coat of PVA glue, which dries clear. Use the paintbrush to smooth out any air bubbles trapped under the scraps.

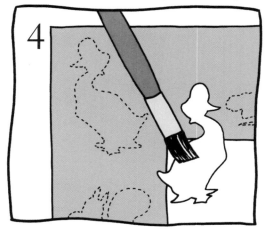

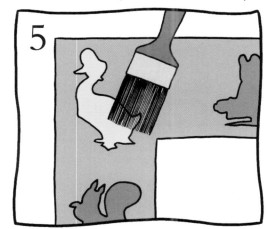

To finish off, apply a light coat of varnish and leave it to dry for at least six hours. Apply approximately three coats of varnish for a durable finish.

Helpful Hints

- Use a colour copier to make more scraps, if necessary.
- Keep paintbrush strokes running in the same direction.
- Add white paint of the same type to lighten a paint colour.
- Remove old paint with stripper or sandpaper.

PICTURE FRAMES

New parents love photographing their baby, so decorate several frames with decoupage scraps.

1. Paint a plain wooden picture frame in a pastel colour.
2. Cut out a decoupage scrap from page 15 and glue it on to lightweight card.
3. Trim around the character, then glue it on to one of the frame's bottom corners.

CLOTHES HANGERS

Details such as decoupage hangers extend the nursery's theme into the wardrobe.

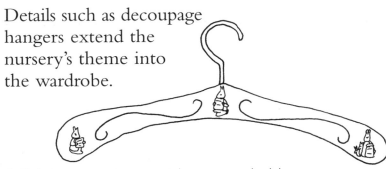

1. Paint a wooden coat hanger pale blue.
2. Position and glue three rabbit scraps from page 18 on the hanger, one in the middle and one at either end.
3. As a finishing touch, paint a wavy, white flourish between each scrap with a thin brush.
4. Allow the paint to dry before varnishing.

COAT PEGS

Customise these useful coat pegs with Beatrix Potter's charming characters.

1. Begin by painting the coat pegs bright, contrasting colours, such as yellow for the backing board and blue for the pegs.
2. Cut out your scraps from page 15, and arrange one character above each coat peg.
3. After gluing the scraps in place and varnishing, mount the coat pegs on the nursery wall.

MIRROR

Young children will be fascinated by their reflection in this mirror, framed with favourite characters.

1. Paint a plain, wooden mirror frame blue.
2. Arrange scraps from page 14 around the frame.
3. Glue the scraps into place, then paint a wavy, white border between the characters.
4. When the paint has dried, varnish the frame.

NAME PLATES

Making a name plate to hang on the nursery door takes just minutes.

KIRSTIE'S ROOM

1. Cut a rectangle of pastel card 6 × 12 cm (2^1/$_2$ × 5 inches).
2. Then cut a smaller rectangle of white paper 4 × 10 cm (1^1/$_2$ × 4 inches) and glue it to the centre of the card.
3. Stick a Peter Rabbit or Jemima Puddle-duck scrap from page 14 to one side of the rectangle.
4. Write your child's name on the white square with letter transfers, stencils or calligraphy. Why not make name plates for any of the baby's siblings?

CHAIR

A comfortable chair is a nursery necessity for late-night feedings and bedtime stories.

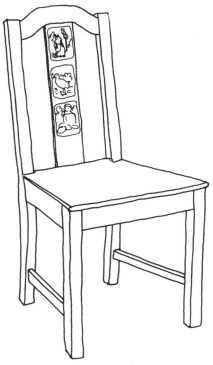

1. Paint a wooden chair pale yellow.
2. Cut out three large, lozenge-shaped scraps from page 19 and position them down the back of the chair.
3. Glue the scraps to the chair and apply several coats of varnish for a lasting, hard-wearing finish.

Your decoupage scraps to cut out can be found overleaf
and on pages 18–19.

Duplicates of most scraps have been provided to allow
for mistakes or making multiple objects.
Why not experiment with your own designs,
using the extra scraps provided? To make additional
decoupage scraps, copy the scrap pages
on a colour photocopier.

Decoupage scraps for Name Plates

Decoupage scraps for Mirror

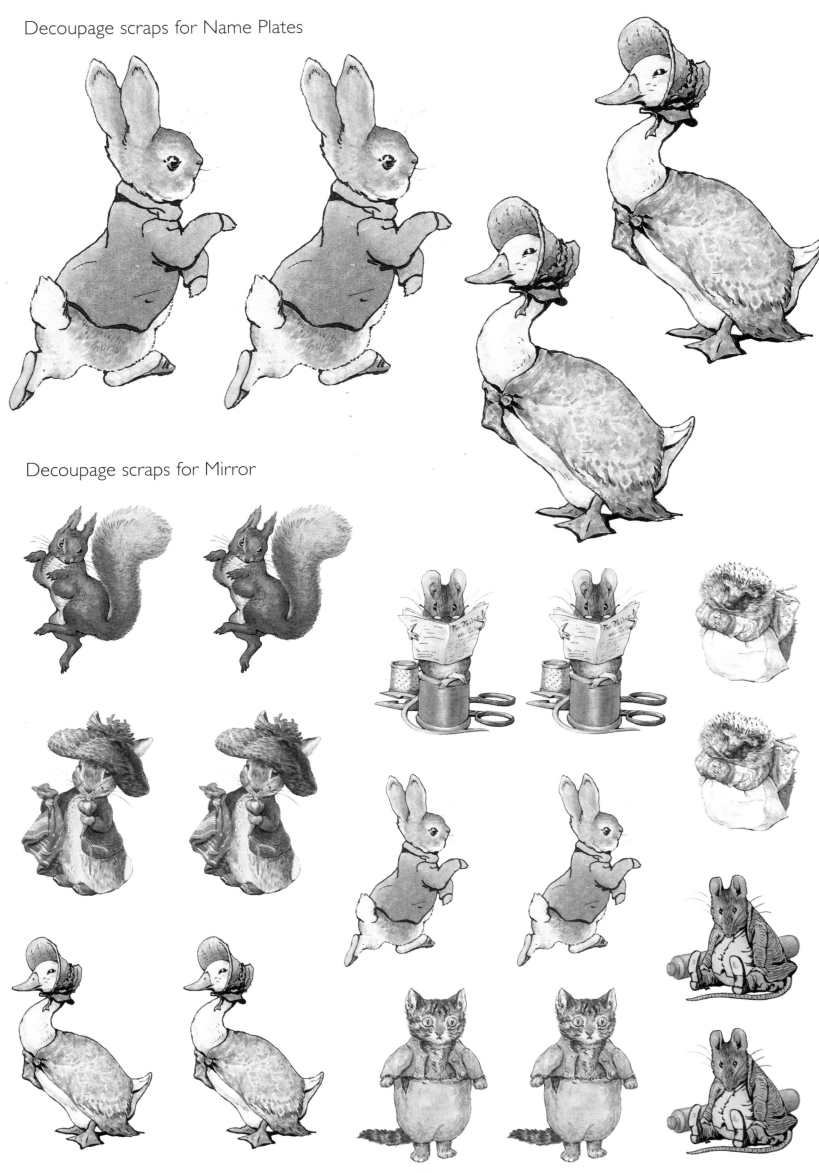

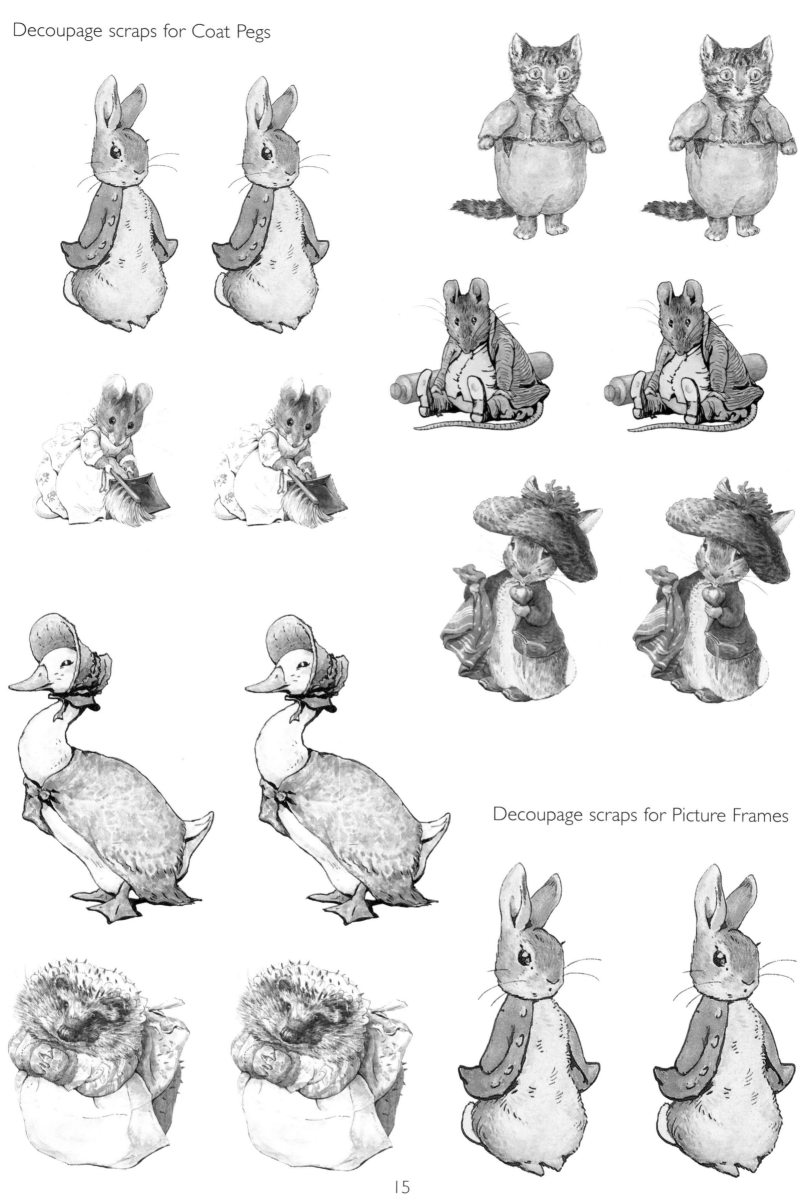

Decoupage scraps for Coat Pegs

Decoupage scraps for Picture Frames

Decoupage scraps for Clothes Hangers

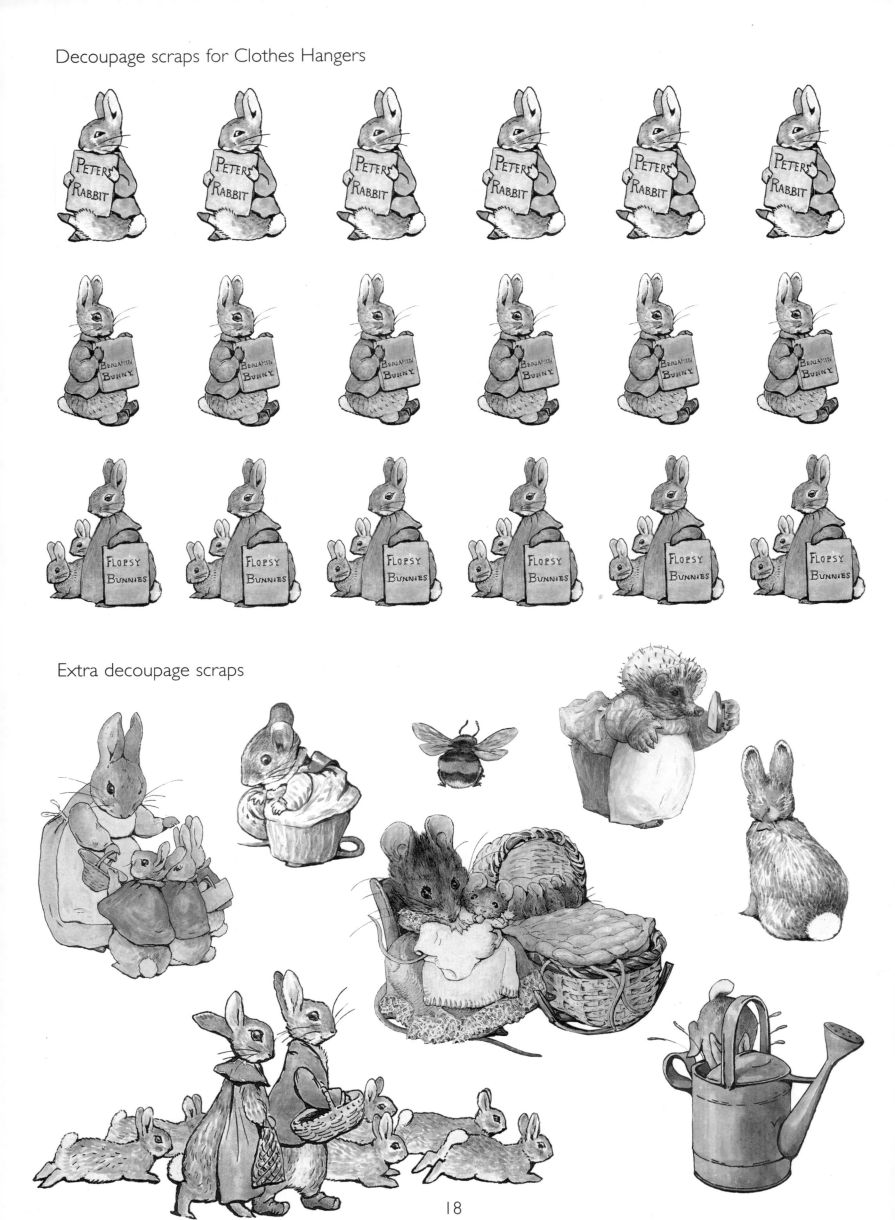

Extra decoupage scraps

Decoupage scraps for Chair

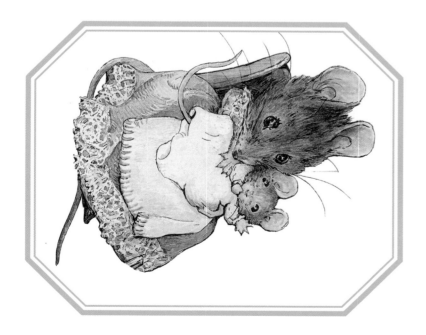

SOFT TOY TECHNIQUES

Sewing soft toys is very satisfying and not as difficult as you might imagine. Familiarise yourself with these techniques if you are new to making soft toys.

Preparation

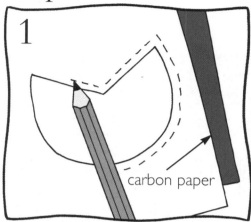

Use carbon paper to trace the pattern pieces on to thick card. Allow an extra 5 mm (¹/₄ inch) all round the pattern pieces for the seams.

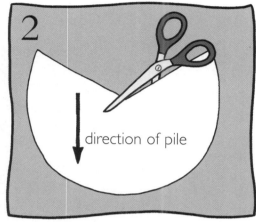

Mark the templates to show the direction of the pile. Draw around the patterns on the back of the fur fabric, then cut out the pieces.

Helpful Hints

- Use high-quality fur fabric to achieve an attractive, hard-wearing result.

- Remember to check that the pile is running in the right direction, particularly when cutting out folded fabric.

- Card templates are sturdier and easier to trace around than paper patterns.

Y stitch

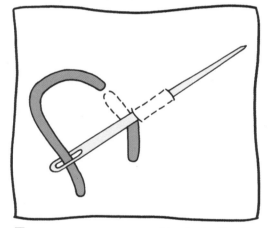

To sew a nose, use a Y stitch. Push the needle through from the base of the head to the tip of the nose. Sew three small stitches in a Y shape.

French knot

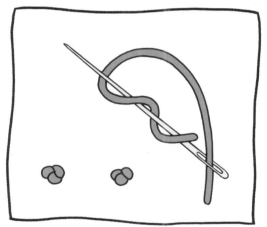

Push the needle through the fabric and wrap the thread around the needle twice. Tighten the twists, turn the needle and reinsert it. Pull tight.

Helpful Hints

- When making soft toys, sew the pattern pieces with the right sides together unless otherwise indicated.

- As you work, clip the curves and corners and trim seams where necessary.

- Use a blunt tool, such as the handle of a spoon or brush, to turn the fabric right-side out.

Whiskers

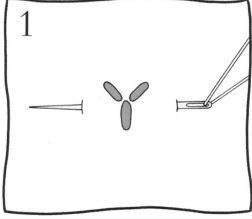

Insert a needle double threaded with fishing line horizontally into the head about 2.5 cm (1 inch) to the side of the nose and push it through.

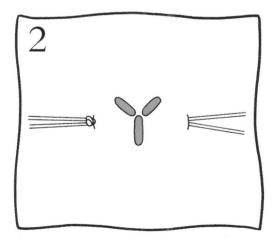

Bring the needle up the same distance from the nose on the opposite side. Leave 5 cm (2 inches) of line protruding from the first side.

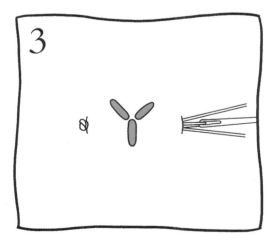

Tie a French knot in the line. Reinsert the needle next to the knot and pull it out close to the whiskers. Trim the ends and repeat on the other side.

PETER RABBIT SOFT TOY

Children become inseparable from their beloved soft toys. Perfect for toddlers, soft toys can withstand the hugs and cuddles lavished upon them without breaking. This fluffy, sturdy Peter Rabbit doll will surely be a favourite.

RABBIT BODY

1. Sew the two ear-liners to the two outer ear pieces, leaving the straight edge open. Turn right side out.

2. Fold the bottom of the ears in at either side so that they meet in the middle and baste in position.

3. Place the front head on top of the back head with edges matching. Fit the ears, ear-liners facing up, between the two head pieces, so that the straight edges fit between the notches. The ears should be sandwiched between the front and back head pieces. Pin the straight edges together and then sew.

4. Pin one of the side head pieces to the front head, matching points **B**, **C** and **D**. Starting from **B**, baste the two pieces together until you come to the bottom of the back head **E**. Do the same with the other side head piece, but leave a gap of 5 cm (2 inches) at the bottom. Now baste together the two side head pieces from **B** to **A** to complete the head shape before sewing properly.

You will need:
- ¹/₂ m (¹/₂ yd) tan fur fabric,
- 23 cm (¹/₄ yd) white fur fabric
- 11.5 cm (¹/₈ yd) white velour
- 2 brown safety eyes
- dark brown embroidery thread
- thick, clear fishing line
- polyester stuffing
- scissors
- needle
- card
- carbon paper

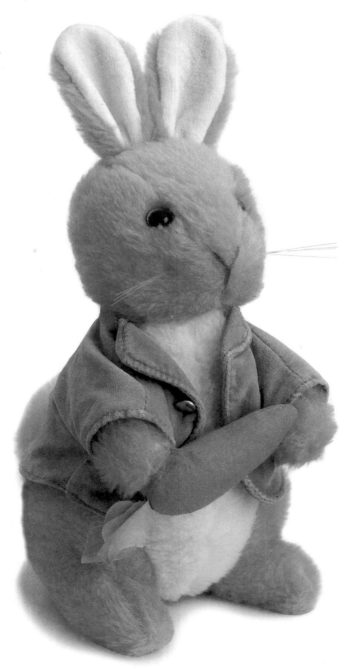

5. Pierce tiny holes at the eye positions with the end of a small pair of sharp scissors. Insert the safety eyes through the holes and secure on the reverse with the metal washers provided.

6. Embroider the nose, using the Y stitch shown on page 21. Each stitch should measure 15 mm (⁵/₈ inch).

7. Sew the darts closed on each side of the head.

8. Place the two front body pieces together and sew the seam **A–B**.

9. Place the two inside arms on either side of the front body, matching the notches (**D**), and sew together. Do the same with the inside legs, but sew only as far as **E**.

10. Match the side bodies to the front body and sew together. Leave the back open.

11. Pin the bottom to the body, matching points **A** at the front and **J** at the sides. Sew all around.

12. Sew the two tail pieces together, leaving the wedge shape open. Turn the tail right side out. Fold it in half, so the two points meet, and sew it between **H** and **I** on the back body.

13. To sew the head on to the body, match notch **C** on the front body to the seam running down the middle of the face and, with right sides together, sew all the way round the neck. Now sew up the gap left at the back of the head.

14. Sew up the back, leaving **F** to **G** open. Turn the rabbit right side out and stuff with polyester stuffing. Sew the back opening closed by hand.

14. Using thick, clear fishing line, sew whiskers on either side of the nose, as shown on page 21.

JACKET

1. Hem across the neckline and bottom of the back jacket.
2. Place the front jacket pieces on the back jacket and sew along the top sleeves of both arms. Hem around the wrists.
3. Sew the darts closed in the front jacket pieces. Then, matching the notches, sew the interfacing (right sides together) to the front jacket pieces. Sew the sides of the jacket closed.
4. Turn the jacket right side out and, starting from the shoulder seam, sew a running stitch about 3 mm ($^1/_8$ inch) in from the edge down the front to the side seam.
5. Fold the top of the front jacket pieces down approximately 2.5 cm (1 inch) from the shoulder to make a lapel and stitch down.
6. Sew the buttons on the right side of the jacket.

You will need:
• 25 cm (10 inches) blue velour
• 2 brass buttons

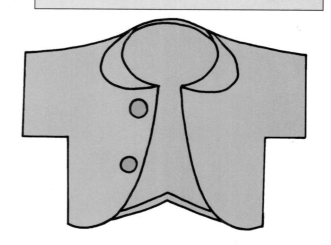

RADISH

1. Fold the leaves in half lengthways, match the straight edge to the top notch of the radish and pin.
2. Fold the radish in half (right sides together) and sandwich the leaves in the middle. Sew round the radish, leaving an opening at one side.
3. Turn the radish right side out and stuff, then hand-sew the opening closed.

You will need:
• 10 × 10 cm (4 × 4 inches) red felt
• scrap of green felt or silk

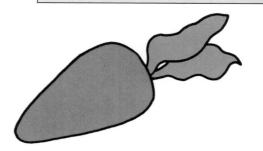

PATTERN PIECES

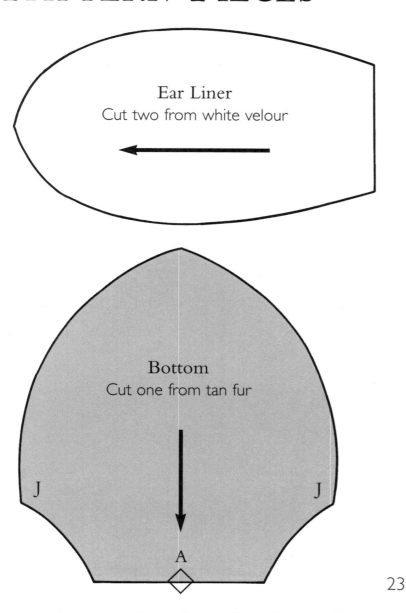

Ear Liner
Cut two from white velour

Bottom
Cut one from tan fur

J   J

A

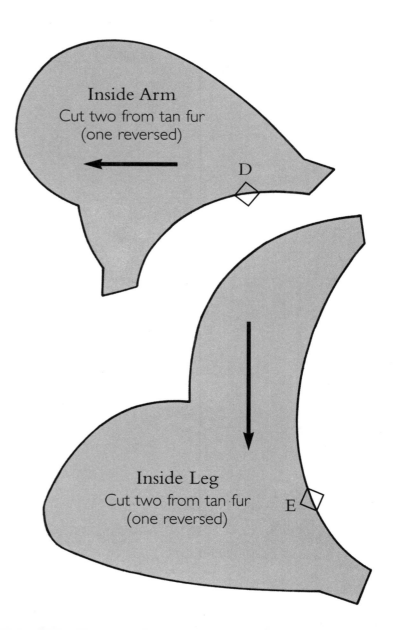

Inside Arm
Cut two from tan fur
(one reversed)

D

Inside Leg
Cut two from tan fur
(one reversed)

E

23

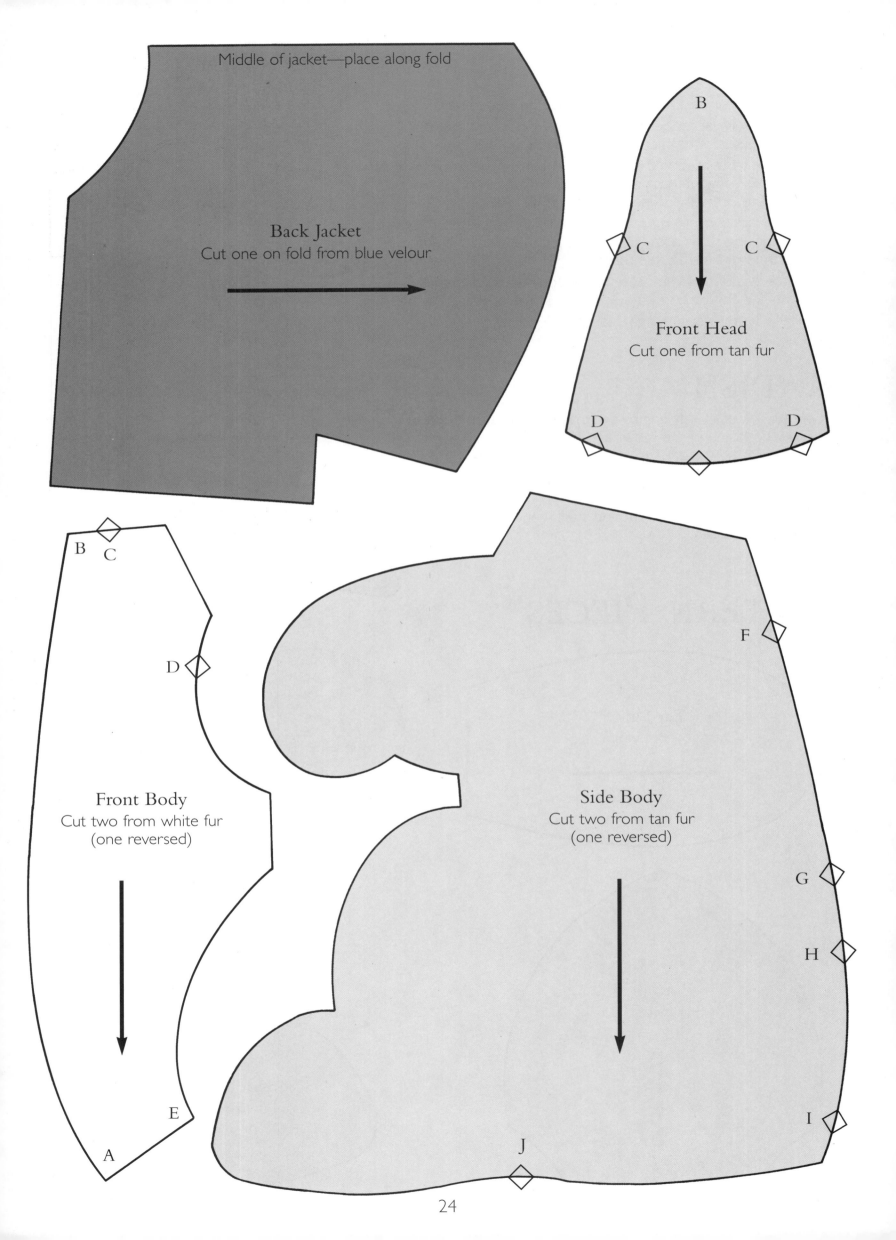

Middle of jacket—place along fold

Back Jacket
Cut one on fold from blue velour

Front Head
Cut one from tan fur

B

C   C

D   D

Front Body
Cut two from white fur
(one reversed)

B C

D

A   E

Side Body
Cut two from tan fur
(one reversed)

F

G

H

I

J

24

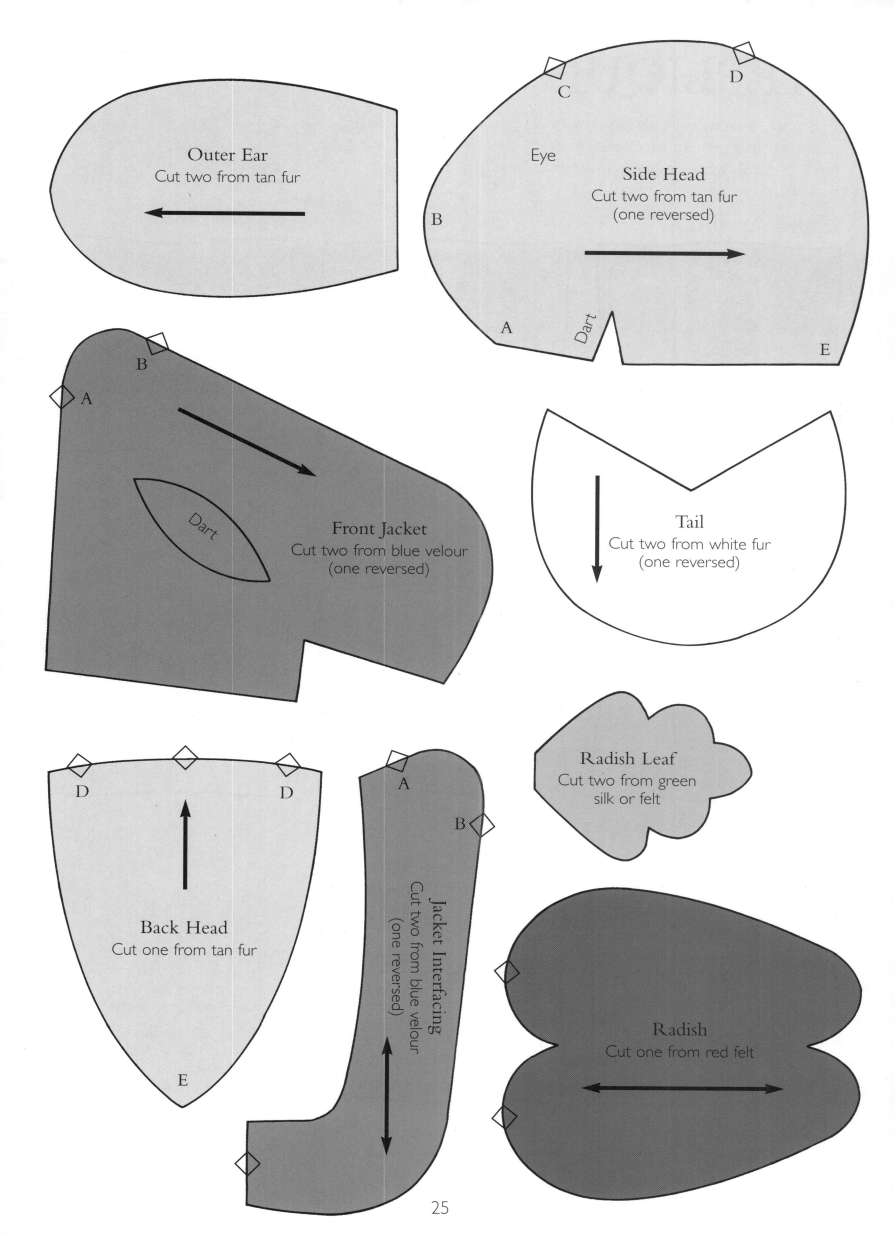

Outer Ear
Cut two from tan fur

Side Head
Cut two from tan fur
(one reversed)

Eye

C

B

D

A

Dart

E

B

A

Dart

Front Jacket
Cut two from blue velour
(one reversed)

Tail
Cut two from white fur
(one reversed)

Radish Leaf
Cut two from green
silk or felt

D

D

A

B

Back Head
Cut one from tan fur

E

Jacket Interfacing
Cut two from blue velour
(one reversed)

Radish
Cut one from red felt

Appliqué

Appliqué, or sewing different fabrics on a background to make colourful images, can be done by hand or using a sewing machine. Even a needlework amateur can create beautiful appliqué wall hangings and soft furnishings.

You will need:
- stencils
- pencil
- seam ripper
- tacking thread
- cotton thread
- pins
- needles
- fabric
- scissors

Hand Appliqué

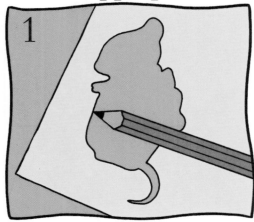

Draw around a stencil on fabric and cut out the shape to make your appliqué piece. Cut out all of the pieces required before sewing.

Pin the appliqué shape in position on the background fabric. Baste it with tacking thread using large, diagonal stitches and smoothing out wrinkles.

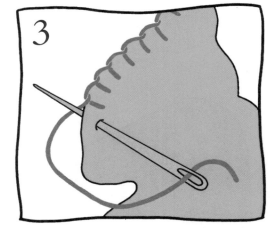

Sew around the shape's edge using tiny, neat buttonhole stitches which produce a secure, decorative edge. Remove tacking with a seam ripper.

Machine Appliqué

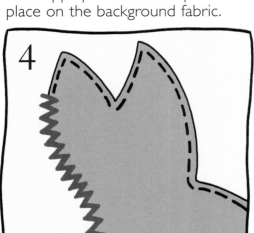

Prepare the appliqué shapes using patterns or stencils, as in step 1 for hand appliqué. Pin the shapes in place on the background fabric.

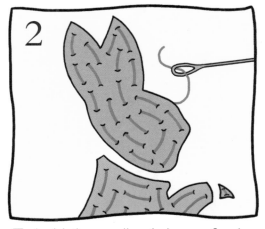

To hold the appliqué shapes firmly in place, baste them with tacking thread. Use long, loose stitches in decreasing, concentric circles.

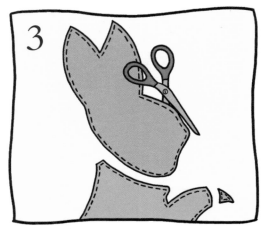

Set your machine to straight stitch and sew around the edges of the appliqué shape. Trim away any excess fabric close to the stitching.

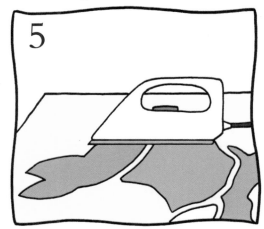

Set your machine to close satin stitch and sew over the straight stitch, making sure to cover the edges of the shape.

Once all of the appliqué shapes have been sewn, remove the tacking stitches using a seam ripper. Iron the finished item.

Helpful Hints

- To sew around curves, stop the machine every few stitches and pivot the fabric as required.

- Choose a needle that corresponds with the thickness of the thread and the weight of the fabric.

Appliqué Projects

Cushion

Embroidered Blanket

Personalise your child's blanket or towel by embroidering their initials and favourite character.

1. Trace around a silhouette stencil on to a white blanket using a soft pencil.

2. For the initials, place a piece of tracing paper over the alphabet on page 29 and draw around the relevant letters. Shade over the back of the outlines in pencil. Place the tracing paper (shaded-side down) on the blanket and draw around the letter outlines to transfer the initials.

3. Thread an embroidery needle with knitting wool or embroidery thread. At one edge of the character's outline, push the needle up through the back of the blanket and down again through the opposite edge of the outline. Continue sewing in the character from edge to edge, working from top to bottom.

4. When the entire character is sewn, embroider the monogram using the same method.

WALL TIDY

Organise baby-care odds and ends in this hand-sewn wall hanging with convenient pockets featuring colourful characters.

You will need:
- sturdy blue and white fabrics
- ¹/₂ m (¹/₂ yd) blue ribbon
- felt of different colours
- matching threads
- 2 rods 42 cm (17 inches) long
- scissors and stencils
- pins and needles

Cut a square of blue, sturdy cotton fabric 55 × 37 cm (22 × 15 inches). Sew a hem of 1.5 cm (²/₃ inch) along all four sides of the fabric.

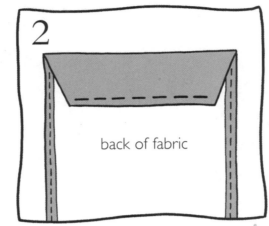

Turn under the top of the fabric about 2.5 cm (1 inch) and stitch along the edge to make a channel. Do the same at the bottom, to make another channel.

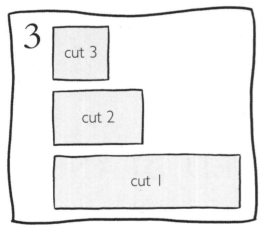

Cut three pieces of white fabric 13 × 13 cm (5 × 5 inches); two pieces 13 × 17 cm (5 × 7 inches); and 1 piece 13 × 35 cm (5 × 14 inches).

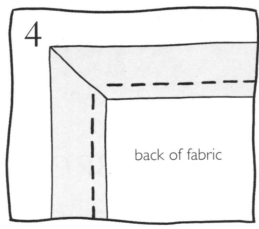

Sew a hem of 1.5 cm (²/₃ inch) on all four sides of each white piece. These pieces of fabric will become the wall tidy's pockets.

Using the silhouette stencils, draw around the characters on different squares of coloured felt. Cut out the characters to make appliqué shapes.

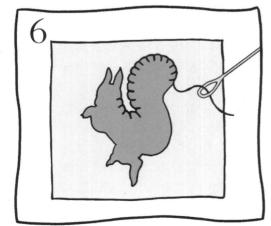

Position character(s) on the front of each pocket. Pin and baste the character shapes, then sew them in place using the hand appliqué method.

Position the pockets on the blue background and pin them in place, as shown. Sew the bottom and side edges of each pocket on to the blue fabric.

Thread a wooden rod through each channel. Tie a length of blue ribbon around each end of the top rod and hang it from a hook on the wall.

CUSHION

Machine appliqué makes this bold Peter Rabbit cushion design quick to sew.

1. Trace the large Peter Rabbit template below on to paper and cut out the pattern pieces. Draw round the pattern pieces on fabric, then cut out your appliqué shapes. Choose brown fabric for Peter's body, blue for his jacket, white for his tail and dark brown for his shoes.

2. Position the appliqué shapes on the centre of a white or cream cushion cover. Pin the pieces into place, then baste them with tacking thread.

3. Sew around the appliqué shapes using straight stitch, then sew over the straight stitch with satin stitch.

4. To make an eye, sew a French knot with dark brown embroidery thread.

5. Measure a frame for the cushion cover, approximately 4 cm (1½ inches) thick, on blue fabric. Cut out the frame and sew it on to the cushion cover, using the machine appliqué technique. Remove the tacking stitches, press the finished cushion cover and insert the cushion.

Peter Rabbit cushion template

A B C D E
F G H I J
K L M N
O P Q R
S T U V
W X Y Z

Trace around your baby's initials to make an embroidery monogram, as shown on page 27.

CLOCK

This easy-to-assemble Tom Kitten clock is not only a practical wall decoration, but it is also a clever toy that will delight young children. Gently pull the ribbon and watch Tom Kitten's arms and legs move.

You will need:
- scissors
- battery-operated clock mechanism and hands
- clock pieces
- 4 paper fasteners
- string and ribbon
- bead

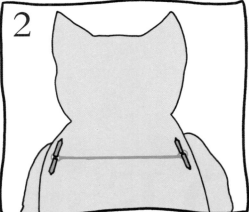

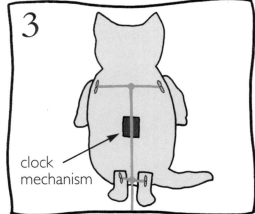

clock mechanism

Cut out the Tom Kitten clock pieces from page 39. Make holes in the card pieces where dots are marked, then match the limbs to the body. Attach the pieces by pushing paper fasteners through both layers.

Open out the fasteners on the back. Tie a piece of string between the top two paper fasteners. Connect the bottom fasteners with string. Attach the clock mechanism to the back of the card and the hands to the front.

Starting at the top, tie a long piece of blue ribbon to the middle of each cross-string, as shown. Thread a bead on to the end of the ribbon and tie it securely in a knot. Mount the clock on the wall.

FRIEZE

This silhouette frieze makes a sweet border for a small bin.

1. Fold a large piece of coloured paper into a concertina. Each fold should be 5.5 cm (2¼ inches) wide.

2. Place a piece of paper over the template opposite and draw around the shape. Shade over the back of the outline in pencil. Place the paper (shaded-side down) on the concertina and draw around the outline to transfer it.

3. Carefully cut around the outline and then open out your frieze. Stick the frieze around the base of a bin or hang it on the nursery wall.

MOBILE

As its colourful cubes and charming characters revolve gently in the breeze, this pretty mobile will fascinate your baby. Follow the simple instructions below to assemble a classic nursery accessory.

You will need:
- scissors
- ruler
- thin ribbon
- glue
- tape

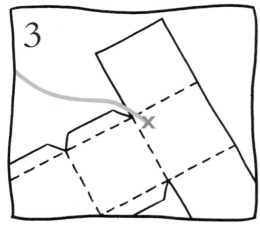

1

Cut out the five mobile pieces, four small and one large, from pages 33–37. Using a ruler or the back of your scissors, score along all the fold lines.

2

Measure and cut four pieces of ribbon 10 cm (4 inches) long. Then cut a longer piece of ribbon, from which to hang the mobile.

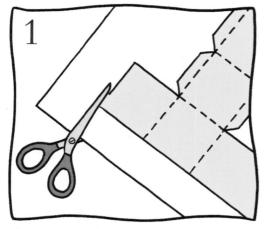

3

Tape a short ribbon to the inside corner of each small mobile piece, as shown. Attach the long ribbon to the inside corner of the large piece.

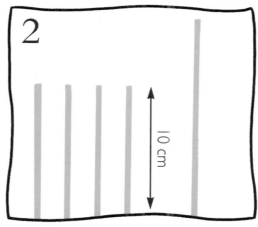

4

glue

Glue along the outside of the flaps. Fold and stick each piece into a cube, tucking the flaps inside and hanging the ribbon outside the cube.

5

When you have finished constructing all five cubes, thread the loose end of a small cube's ribbon through the eye of a darning needle.

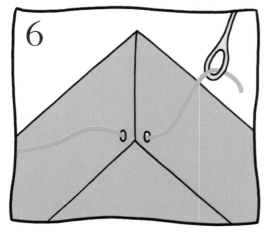

6

Push the needle through any of the large cube's corners, except the one with the long ribbon. Pull the ribbon through and tie the end in a knot.

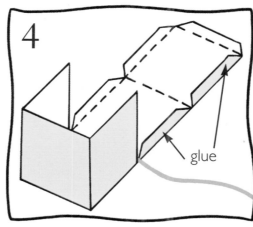

7

Repeat steps five and six for each small cube. Each of the four small cubes should dangle from a different corner of the large cube, as shown.

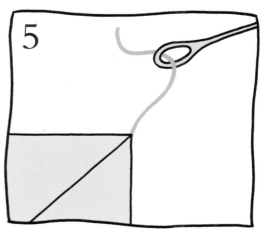

8

Hang the finished mobile by tying the long ribbon to a ceiling hook. Watch as this adorable nursery decoration turns round in the air.

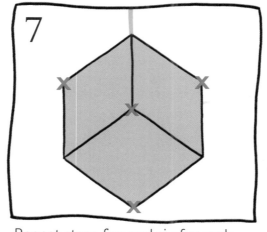

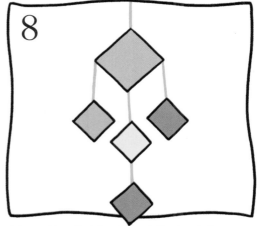

FREDERICK WARNE
Published by the Penguin Group
Penguin Books Ltd, 27 Wrights Lane, London W8 5TZ, England
Penguin Putnam Inc., 375 Hudson Street, New York, NY 10014, USA
Penguin Books Australia Ltd, Ringwood, Victoria, Australia
Penguin Books Canada Ltd, 10 Alcorn Avenue, Toronto, Ontario, Canada M4V 3B2
Penguin Books (N.Z.) Ltd, 182-190 Wairau Road, Auckland 10, New Zealand

Penguin Books Ltd, Registered Offices: Harmondsworth, Middlesex, England

First published 1999 by Frederick Warne

1 3 5 7 9 10 8 6 4 2

ISBN 0 7232 4487 1

Photography by Steve Shott
Additional illustrations by Kirstie Billingham and Eliz Hüseyin
Design by Kirstie Billingham
Text by Anne Marie Ryan
Special thanks to Lorna Penfound for appliqué consultancy and to Susannah Willis for modelling

Colour reproduction by Saxon Photolitho Ltd., Norwich
Printed in Singapore by Imago Publishing Ltd.